india

india

decoration | interiors | design

Henry Wilson

conran OCTOPUS

Dedicated to those who introduced me to India and supported and encouraged me from my early days.

First published in 2001 by
Conran Octopus Limited
A part of Octopus Publishing Group
2–4 Heron Quays
London E14 4JP
www.conran-octopus.co.uk

This paperback edition published in 2006

ISBN 1 84091 464 5

Publishing Director Lorraine Dickey
Commissioning Editor Emma Clegg
Copy Editor Barbara Mellor
Proofreader Barbara Roby
Indexer Peter Barber

Creative Director Leslie Harrington
Executive Art Editor Megan Smith

Production Director Zoe Fawcett
Senior Production Controller Manjit Sihra

Artworks drawn by Henry Wilson from original architectural and interior motifs

British Library Cataloguing-in-Publication Data
A catalogue record for this book is available from the British Library

Printed in China

first page Detail of a wood block-printed design taken from a piece of antique fabric. **previous pages left** New embroidered leather jutis (slippers) hang on the walls of a cobbler's shop. Ahmedabad, Gujarat. **previous pages right** The interior of a Bohra terraced house in the town of Siddhpur, Gujarat. **opposite** Terracotta and brass water pots in a village house in Saurashtra district, Gujarat.

contents

पाकीज़ा
TIKAMDAS DAYALDAS & SONS
टीकमदास दयालदास एण्ड सन्स
स्वीट्स
खट्टन बीड़ी
"मज़ा लिया
तेज का
भूली सारी
रामायण
तेज ही चाय
पाकीज़ा
TIKAMDAS DAYALDAS & SONS
टीकमदास दयालदास एण्ड सन्स
स्वीट्स
खट्टन बीड़ी

culture & design

Pencil-sharpening and procrastination must be the twin banes of anyone attempting to write anything that endeavours to embrace India in its entirety. It just is not possible. Even the great travel writers have been floored by the extraordinary cornucopia that is India: writers such as Hsuän Tsang from seventh-century China, the Frenchmen Bernier in the seventeenth century and Rousselet in the twentieth, and the Englishmen Colonel Todd, Bishop Heber and Kipling in the nineteenth century, to name only a few. All have been amazed and exhilarated by the diversity of India, and by its wondrous buildings and the exquisite skills of its painters, decorators and craftsmen and women. Not least among these travellers was the American writer Mark Twain, who journeyed to India in the late nineteenth century to describe it for a curious audience back home. He soon realized just what a monumental task he had undertaken: 'When you think you have come to the end of her tremendous specialties and have finished hanging tags upon her as … the Land of the Plague, the Land of Famine, the Land of Giant Illusions, the Land of Stupendous Mountains and so forth, another specialty crops up and another tag is required.' In the end, he concluded that no less ambitious a title than 'Land of Wonders' would suffice.

India's history is so wide-ranging and ancient as to be overwhelming: archaeological excavations in Gujarat have revealed evidence of settlements dating back to 3000 BC; indeed, India contains the oldest living city in the world, the holy Hindu city of Varanasi. Whereas most of the world's continents can boast one major empire or civilization, India has bred a multitude, including the great Buddhist empire of Ashoka and the medieval Hindu empire in the south. From the sixteenth century, the great Mughal dynasty reigned from Delhi in the north, before the British arrived to make Calcutta in the east the second city of their world empire. Only since 1947 has India been its own unified master.

All this history and culture are bounded by one of the longest coastlines in the world. Within this natural boundary lies a breathtaking variety of landscapes and habitats, including the world's highest mountains and areas of greatest rainfall; parched deserts and teeming rainforests; great rivers that meander so shallowly to the coast that each year they bring devastating floods; arcadian pockets such as the valley of Kashmir, sitting in the cupped palms of the Himalayas; miles of coastline that produce one of the great staples of life, salt; and fertile lands that grow spices for the world, and which in the sixteenth and seventeenth centuries attracted the attentions of European maritime adventurers like bees to a honey pot.

Much of India's culture and wealth has been influenced and created by trade, and the subcontinent has for centuries been criss-crossed by trade routes. One of the most famous, still in existence after hundreds of years and now more congested than ever, is the 'Grand Trunk Road' which crosses the country from the Pakistan border in the west to Calcutta in the east. Nor were trade routes confined to the land, for India also boasts an ancient tradition of navigation on the high seas, with redoubtable merchant adventurers developing huge fortunes. The togas worn by Roman senators were made from Indian cotton, and scraps of cloth of Indian origin dating from around the

left An assorted collection of posters illustrating various Hindu gods, including Shiva, Krishna, Ganesh and Hanuman on the wall of the night watchman's room at the Chanwar Palki Walon-Ki haveli, Amber, near Jaipur.

ninth century have been found in Lower Egypt; much later, some of the battleships for Nelson's Trafalgar fleet were built in India from Indian wood. Not surprisingly, foreign merchants and adventurers yearned to investigate the source of this trade and discover the wealth they presumed it must have created. Thus it was that trade, with its accompanying exposure to the wider world and to other societies and cultures, attracted waves of the inquisitive and the avaricious – including the Mughal, Portuguese, Dutch, French and British – over hundreds of years.

Such epic comings and goings have left their mark on India, and are most immediately visible in the country's architectural legacy: Lord Curzon, British viceroy from 1898–1905, declared that India possessed 'the greatest galaxy of monuments in the world'. Today its architecture encompasses an extraordinary variety of forms and styles, reflecting differences in climate and religion, as well as the legacy of numerous invaders and colonizers. Before these cultural and physical invasions, however, India had already developed its own distinctive styles. Examples of these are evident in the painted caves of Ajanta from the Buddhist period (third to fifth centuries AD), or the Hindu southern capital of Vijayanagara (*c*1350–1565). But so much of India's distinctive architecture owes it unique character to a cross-fertilization of cultures, marrying the Mughal with the Rajput, Muslim concepts with Hindu craftsmanship, Hindu styles with British tastes. The results of this cultural journey now encompass architectural extremes, from the simplest of human habitations, the indigenous roundhouse, to the ultimate in sophistication, elegance and artistry, as represented by the Mughal Taj Mahal. Perhaps more than any other country, India has absorbed a huge diversity of

opposite A man meditates on his rosary, seated on a terrace high above the Ganges River, Varanasi. **above far left** A woman stands stoically against the autumn dawn chill proffering a puja lamp as she awaits the appearance of Lord Surya, the sun god, Varanasi, Uttar Pradesh. **above left** On the day of the full moon at the end of the Kartik month, crowds converge to bathe at Panchaganga Ghat, Varanasi. **left** Akash Deep, the 'sky lantern festival'. Throughout the autumn month of Kartik, wicker lanterns are lit at dusk and dawn to aid the visiting spirits of the dead to find their way to the other world.

above and below left In the urban environment colour and design are to be found wherever you turn your head; whether it be piles of dye powder; design on the most mundane of domestic packaging; the exterior of giant 'All-India' haulage truck cabins; mudguards on auto-rickshaws; political graffiti; film hoardings, and religious shrines and temples. The urban street is a visual cacophony of advertising boards and cloth banners as each shop, large and small, vies for customers' attention. Colour and design touch every part of life in a country where the visitors' senses are sent soaring, additionally provoked by boundless sound, smell and motion.

the Bohras were heavily influenced by British urban styles of the period, not only in the architecture they favoured, but also in the layout, decoration and furnishings of their own homes.

The façades of their houses were considered the ideal place for a proud display of wealth and success; embellished with baroque and art deco designs and painted in candyfloss colours, they indicate nothing of the Muslim culture of the inhabitants. Each house frontage included a plaque bearing the family monogram, usually positioned beside the front door, applied in relief and picked out in colour, following a European tradition imported by the British. The entwined initials of the family were combined with those of the city in which they had established their businesses, and in some cases, the families also adopted the name of that city, so creating titles such as Calcuttawalla and Adenwalla.

Each house is entered across a raised threshold with a small sitting area in front of the main door, while the front room is shielded from public view by an Edwardian-style screen set with glass panels that are hand-painted with landscapes of the Ponte Vecchio or Mount Fuji, copied with some licence by local artists from postcards. Inside, the full extent of foreign influence becomes clear. Gone is the traditional open courtyard, in favour of a narrow air well for ventilation; the traditional mud floor has been replaced with tiles, smart and easy to maintain, laid in repeating geometric patterns; and dados painted with local scenes have been replaced with European-style decorative tiles. Guests are entertained formally in the drawing room at the back of the building, where mattresses covered with white sheets and lavish Persian-style rugs mark a return to tradition. Built-in cupboards in Burmese teak double as storage space and display cabinets, their elaborate carving, frequently crowned with extravagant crests, again echoing European aristocratic grandeur.

The merchant houses of Ahmedabad differ from those of Siddhpur and Shekhavati in a number of respects, and not least in their setting. The origins of the former capital of Gujarat stretch back as far as the eleventh century, and the old walled city is congested and compact. In contrast to the freestanding mansions of the Marwaris or the rigorous grid layout of the Bohra 'new town', the Ahmedabad havelis seem buried in a labyrinth of lanes and gullies. In former centuries, Ahmedabad was a thriving production centre for many commodities, including weapons and above all

above left The Bohra terraced houses are notable for their consistent architectural structure. The surface decoration, however, presents a mixture of styles, the most popular being art deco.

above right A Bohra mother and daughter prepare to go shopping. The women are not obliged to cover their faces in public, unlike the custom in some Indian communities.

above left The main courtyard of the Manganbhai haveli in the old quarter of Ahmedabad in Gujarat.
above right Whether substantial or small, every Ahmedabad haveli has carved ornamentation on their wood frontages.

textiles. The city's climate made it ideal for cotton work, so that when the British arrived it became a focus for industrialization. At its peak, it boasted over fifty cotton mills, each employing some four to five thousand workers, from which it became known as the 'Manchester of the East'. Many grand havelis were built from the profits of this trade, but inevitably the mill owners began to forsake the crowded old city for new mansions which could incorporate all the latest comforts and conveniences. As a consequence, many of their old homes in the walled city were left deserted.

Although neglected for so many years, the buildings remain intact thanks to their method of construction. While the houses of Siddhpur and Shekhavati were primarily of stone, the Ahmedabad mansions were built half of brick and half of wood, the dry climate that favoured cotton also favouring timber production. When local supplies ran out, wood was imported from the Spice Coast in southern India and as far away as Burma.

The havelis are frequently raised above street level, with verandas running the width of the frontage. Above the veranda is a cantilevered upper floor, further supported by either an elegantly proportioned wooden arcade set in stone, or by beautifully carved struts. Skilled wood-block cutters from the textile industry probably also worked on the havelis: the carved woodwork of the façades is certainly as fine as that required for block prints. Artisans from both the Hindu and the Muslim communities worked on these mansions in a spirit of intense rivalry, their different styles and subject matter leading to tremendous diversity in their work. The deeply carved supporting struts of the upper storeys are exquisitely worked with mythical creatures and flowing floral motifs. On the upper floors, architraves and rafters are a riot of intricate design, including flowers, leaves, creepers, carved elephants, peacocks and – virtually an unofficial emblem of India – cheeky emerald-green parrots.

The mansions of the Shekhavati district in northern Rajasthan belong to the families of the Marwari business community who today hold centre stage in the rapidly expanding economy of modern India. Initially, they made their fortunes from the trade caravans that criss-crossed their region on the way to and from Delhi: south to the Arabian Sea and on to Africa, west to present-day Pakistan and on to Iran, and north to Kabul in Afghanistan. Later, the British arrived in the guise of the East India Company, and land-based trade routes withered as the colonialists

established the great sea ports of Calcutta and Bombay. The shrewd Marwaris moved to the new ports, and particularly to Calcutta, where they now form the single biggest, wealthiest and most influential section of the population. Under the British they became agents, brokers and financiers in the sea ports, specializing in commodities such as opium, tea, jute, silver and gold. A portion of the fabulous wealth accrued by the Marwari merchants was sent back to the homeland, where it was used to finance the building of magnificent havelis.

In the late nineteenth century, a feverish passion for new building gripped the Marwaris, in tandem with a craze for fresco painting, all provoked by the heady spirit of one-upmanship that now consumed the merchants. Fresco painting is a traditional skill in Rajasthan, and as the new buildings went up, local artists were offered large, fresh canvases to work on. Each haveli had to be bigger and better and each fresco brighter and more refined than the next one. Every local artist was dragooned into service, reinforcements were brought in from all over the state as well as from neighbouring ones, and the wealthiest merchants lured the most talented court painters to come and work on their mansions.

In such a competitive climate, the owners were not particularly concerned with the subject matter of the paintings, and therefore gave the artists free rein. Their chief artistic inspiration came from religion, but they also depicted kings and queens and their courts, everyday scenes of women collecting water, hunting scenes, floral and geometric motifs and portraits of animals such as elephants and camels. The subject matter also reflected the changing times. Through the sea ports, the Marwari merchants were exposed to the world beyond India, and more particularly to the wonders of the Industrial Revolution. On their annual visits to their desert mansions they took back lithographs and drawings of marvels such as steam-driven trains and ships, horse-drawn landaus and Mr Ford's new four-wheeled contraption, which were duly included – in delightfully incongruous fashion – in the frescoes on their walls. The chemical reaction between the water-based pigments and the lime plaster of the walls has lent the frescoes a surprising degree of permanence despite the glaring sunlight of the location. Because the pigment was applied to the damp plaster the artists had to work very fast before the plaster dried, creating a distinctively fluid and spontaneous style.

above left A night watchman sits in front of his haveli in the Shekhavati district. **above centre** Many of the grand fresco-decorated havelis in the Shekhavati district have been abandoned, the owners now living in the large cities. **above right** The haveli entrances have elegant cusped arches and are furnished with heavy, solid doors.

bohras of siddhpur

The Bohras of Siddhpur created a new business empire for themselves in the early twentieth century. One result of this was a magnificent new town in Gujarat. One of the avenues running off the central mall clearly shows the somewhat incongruous influence of British metropolitan style, as filtered through the Raj. Bohra dwellings were influenced by European tastes in both their design and their decoration, as may be seen in the furniture and intricate plasterwork.

opposite The creation of a new quarter in the old town of Siddhpur was strikingly constructed along a grid pattern with long, orderly streets. It presents an incongruous sight in Gujarat, with broad pavements and a strict continuity of façade. **left** Many of the frontages of the Bohra terraced houses were wholly influenced by the deco style. So much were the Bohras taken by the prevailing fashion, that the façades are devoid of any indication of the ethnic character of the owners.

opposite One of the most distinctive features of a Bohra front room is the hitchkar. This swinging seat comes in many styles, depending on the period of its construction. This example is seen in its basic functional form of a slab of wood with a mattress and brass rods, although hitchkars often have highly decorated seats, with carved wood and inset tiles.

above Wood-carved screens tended to be inset with sandblasted or acid-etched glass. The ceiling is decorated with fine plasterwork in European styles and the magnificent carved wood balustrade effects a new formality and grandness also indebted to a European influence. Mass-produced tiles cover the floor with geometric designs.

left The focal point of a Bohra house is the place where the drinking water is kept. The first thing a guest is offered when they visit a Gujarati household is a glass of water. Stored in mutkas, terracotta pots that sweat, the high ambient temperature causes evaporation, which keeps the water deliciously cool. Raised to the point of sanctity, it is often stored in what looks like a shrine. **right** A detail of the intricate plasterwork ceiling. Picking out the plasterwork with painted colours was a matter of taste and not done in every case. **artwork** A detail taken from the plaster relief work bordering the main ceiling.

right The Bohra householder was not afraid to use colour, representing the arrival of the Industrial Revolution, when new synthetic, permanent and industrially made pigments became available. The Bohras, whose business took them far away and overseas, would have been exposed to the new fashion for colour. The mass-produced metal-framed bed, introduced by the British, soon began to replace the traditional wood-framed and string-bottomed charpoy.

left Bulbous European-style swags in plasterwork hang from the cornice, while ornate wood-framed mirrors with decorative crowns dominate the walls. The European influence is evident throughout, from the 1950s period fabric on the sofas to the Aubusson-style rug. **below** The formal drawing room is on the ground floor at the back of the house. It shows a partial return to tradition in the mode of seating with bolster cushions against the walls. The expensive Indian rug is generally covered with calico to protect it from dust and sunlight.

far left and below The plaster-decorated ceilings are a distinctive feature of the Bohra interior. Like the Marwaris in Shekhavati, the Bohras were traders in the great sea ports but also went much further afield. One Bohra reached such heights of wealth and influence in the court of Emperor Haile Selassi in Addis Ababa, Ethiopia, that he became known as the 'Uncrowned King of Ethiopia'. **above left** This mirror-fronted door decorated with fruit, birds and flowers has a distinct feel of the Ottoman Empire. **opposite** The Taj Mahal is justly a source of great pride in a Muslim household. Madraswalla is the family name, adopted from Madras, the city in which their business thrived.

MADRASWALLA

wooden havelis of ahmedabad

It was said that Ahmedabad hung on three threads: gold, silver and cotton. The earliest of the city's wooden havelis date from the fifteenth century, and for many years these were the homes of the city's rich merchants, who created immense wealth. The most profitable of their numerous business activities were based on cotton, textiles and particularly the indigo dye for which the city was famous. The exquisite mansions still stand, hidden in the labyrinth of the old city, their flamboyant displays of fine wood-carving surviving as an outward sign of the status, grandeur and discerning taste of their erstwhile owners.

opposite The main courtyard of a haveli. A tissue-paper kite hangs from the rooftop – kite flying and fighting is a popular pastime, particularly in January when the festival of Uttran takes place. **below left** It might be assumed that these grand mansions, buried deep in the heart of the old city, would be suffocatingly hot in summer, but the worst of the heat is kept at bay with cross-ventilation, ventilation shafts, deep courtyards and the hitchkar. **below right** All the interaction with the outside world took place in the first courtyard of the haveli, entered directly from the street. This is where the very best of the wood-carved façades would be positioned, letting any visitor know that the merchant was wealthy and successful.

opposite and left The façade of the merchant's haveli facing the street was reserved for the finest of the decorative wood-carving. The city had a tradition of carving through its position as a centre for textiles, whose fabric printing demanded the highest standard of craftsmanship in the carving of wood blocks. This skill could be adapted for the decoration of the havelis. There was energetic competitiveness between the merchants and the craftsmen themselves to have the most florid and exquisitely carved façades. **artwork** Taken from a carved wooden panel façade on one of the grand merchants' havelis.

frescoes of shekhavati

The painted façades of the handsome and imposing havelis that make up the desert towns of the Shekhavati district of northern Rajasthan are unmistakable. Built for Marwari merchants as impressive displays of their wealth, they are painted inside and out with a remarkable gallery of frescoes on religious, royal and everyday themes. Nowhere else in India, or indeed the world, boasts such prolific amounts of fresco work. The colourful decoration forms a strong contrast with the drab surroundings of scrub desert where temperatures soar to fifty degrees centigrade in summer and plummet below zero in winter.

previous pages left The flat, smooth finish of the grand stone mansions of Shekhavati was perfect to paint on rather than carve. **previous pages right** The havelis would accommodate the extended family; three generations, along with various family branches, lived in a single haveli. A rivalry gripped the merchant families who competed with each other to have the biggest and most exuberantly frescoed building.

left and opposite The haveli frescoes were painted over a period of three-hundred years and richly illustrate social change and developments in lifestyle, particularly during the nineteenth century. There was a fascination for the products of the Industrial Revolution, such as the steam boat and steam train, the car and the Wright brothers' first airplane. Alongside these quirky images were more localized subjects: shikars (tiger hunts), Royal Durbars, portraits of princes and religious subjects.

left The finest fresco work was reserved for the interior and the richer the merchant the better the artists he could afford. No surface was left untouched and this included awkward ceilings. Producing a fresco involves creating a chemical reaction between the water-based pigment and the lime plaster, so painting had to be quickly completed while the plaster was still wet. This resulted in a free-style form of illustration. **opposite** The entrance to a merchant's haveli is where some of the finest frescoes can be found. The ferengi (foreigner) was a frequent subject: the topi wallas (hat men) and their barra sahibs (foreign ladies) with their crinolines and parasols. **artwork** Border detail taken from one of the painted havelis of Shekhavati.

opposite Not only did these merchants build extravagant homes, but they paid for buildings and facilities for the wider community. They believed that this would guarantee them a place in heaven so they did not stint on the quality. Temples and shrines were as exquisitely painted as their own houses, with religious scenes and illustrations of Indian mythology, shown here through the interior of the dome of a temple. **below** An example of the exuberance of the fresco painters of the nineteenth century, this ceiling has been covered with geometric and floral motifs. The band of portraits consist of rose-cheeked, white-faced ladies and gentlemen in refined clothes. All of the characters wear hats, which were strongly associated with these foreigners.

forts & palaces

| samode palace | neemrana fort | udai bilas palace | devi garh fort |

above left Samode Palace rests at the end of a valley in the Aravalli hills outside Jaipur. The imposing façade symbolized the ruler's power. **above centre** Three kilometres from the palace, Samode Bagh is a garden paradise recently restored by the current family. **above right** Dancers from the Kabalia caste perform for guests in the exquisitely decorated durbar hall of the palace.

artwork on page 42 Detail of the cut-glass mosaic work in the Udai Bilas Palace, Dungarpur. **previous page** Detail of the painted walls of the hall behind the Sultan Mahal, Samode Palace.

As recently as fifteen years ago the royal palaces of India appeared doomed. It seemed that four hundred years of glory, despotism, wealth, intrigue, loyalty and service had finally come to an end. These magnificent structures had become millstones round the necks of the families whose ancestors had built and defended them, and their very fabric was crumbling as they became home to monkeys and bats. But as tourism grew, many owners shed their shyness of business in the cause of preserving this unique architecture. The greatest concentration of forts and palaces is to be found in the state of Rajasthan, where they were built by the warrior clan of Rajputs, the Kshatriya caste. Samode Palace near Jaipur, Neemrana near Delhi, and Udai Bilas and Devi Garh, both close to Udaipur, are four Rajasthani palaces that once seemed certain to vanish for ever. They have been saved by returning to their fine tradition of hospitality, receiving guests once more, but now in return for payment.

For centuries Rajasthan and its maharajas have exercised a fascination over foreign imaginations, inspiring stories of rivers of blood, of women throwing themselves on the funeral pyres of their husbands rather than submit to enemy capture, of wild excess and generosity, of intrigue and betrayal, of codes of honour, devotion and loyalty, of sybaritic pleasure and extravagant piety. The maharajas of Rajasthan were all this and more. Two hundred years ago only a handful of foreigners were able to witness a few glimpses of this extraordinary and mysterious world. Richly embellished descriptions of an earthly paradise travelled back to the West, and the fascination of the world of the maharajas continues to draw visitors today.

The geology of Rajasthan is the oldest in the world, making for a wild and forbidding landscape. Even a century ago, travel was arduous, slow, and in high summer almost unbearable. After days of discomfort on dangerous roads, the sudden view of one of these fortified palaces must have been wondrous. More often than not they cling to the side of a boulder-strewn hillside, monumental fortified citadels with sheer walls crowned by crenellated battlements and embellished with clusters of chattris (domed pavilions) and jharokas (decorated covered balconies). Not unlike the great cathedrals of medieval Europe, these Rajput palaces had the effect of instilling awe and respect in those who surveyed them, their sheer bulk and height indicating the power and authority of an absolute ruler.

The arrival of visitors was never unexpected. Days beforehand, the maharaja would be informed – either by guards posted along the way or by heliograph (mirror

telegraph) – of imminent arrivals, when visitors of sufficiently elevated status would be granted an audience with the potentate in the durbar hall, the main public reception room. The full durbar protocol afforded the most effective occasion for the maharaja to display the regal pomp and ceremony that emphasized his power. Tales of such audiences describe the maharaja seated on an elevated gaddi (throne) beneath a gold-embroidered and bejewelled velvet parasol, looking down upon his royal household and a multitude of aristocrats. Smouldering braziers filled the durbar hall with a mist of aromatic incenses, and palace retainers sprinkled the assembled audience with headily perfumed rose water. Foreign visitors were both thrilled and overawed, not only by the assembled royalty but also by the decorative splendour of the durbar halls.

Samode Palace is not only one of the most exquisite creations of its period but also one of the finest of all the Rajput palaces, and its breathtaking durbar hall lives up to every expectation. Of particular brilliance are its painted walls and ceilings, created under Rawal Berisal Singh in the mid-nineteenth century. The Sultan Mahal is an exquisite example of the Jaipur miniature style at its best, with every inch meticulously painted with geometric and floral motifs; the dados represent garden borders filled with flowers and mango trees and inhabited by a profusion of every species of bird found in the region. The rulers of this desert state loved gardens, and this hall brings the delights of an imaginary garden inside.

In the 1970s there seemed little future for Samode, as for so many other palaces, but then its two youthful heirs, Rawal Raghavendra Singh and his brother Rawal Yadavendra Singh, took on the task of saving the property and opened it to a discerning public. Slowly, with considerable thought, sensitivity and integrity, they have returned the huge palace to its former splendour, rightly assuring it a place of honour among India's heritage hotels.

To the north-east of Samode lies the hill of Neemrana. Perched on a natural plateau midway up the steep slopes is a fortified palace, built in the mid-fifteenth century. After Independence it became impossible to maintain such large structures: in 1946 an entire wing had collapsed, and in the 1950s the heirs could not maintain what was left. The deterioration continued for another twenty-five years, until Aman Nath and Francis Wacziarg stumbled across the ruin and, with two other like-minded people, bought it.

The palace complex had been vandalized and all its architectural details pilfered, rooms lay open to the sky and floors had subsided. The new owners wanted to turn it into

above left Neemrana Fort, viewed from the village below. Both a royal home and a fortress, its high position and strong ramparts reflect the importance of its defensive role. **above right** A stone soldier in a cusped arch marks a staircase that leads up to the main body of the fort.

above left A pavilion rises out of the main courtyard of Udai Bilas Palace, Dungarpur. Built in the Indo-Saracenic style, it was once linked by a bridge to the main building. **above right** The palace looks out over Lake Gaibsagar, which is an important centre of migratory birds in winter.

a hotel, but first had to clean up the rubble and shore up the walls before even beginning rebuilding work. Passionately interested in India's architectural and craft heritage, Aman and Francis have become spirited protagonists of a growing movement to rescue what is left of India's heritage: as Aman says, 'saving historical architecture picked from the national dustbin'.

Today Neemrana encapsulates Aman and Francis's design ethos, innovative in spirit and monastic in ambience. Inveterate hunters after antique furniture and bespoke accessories, they are keen to encourage traditional craftsmanship. Each room has been furnished with unique pieces of furniture and elegant hand block-printed fabrics. Aman chose the colonial-style furniture, explaining that 'it has the whimsy of the Indian craftsmen in their interpretation of the European originals: the native workmen rarely knew when to stop'.

The early twentieth century saw a flurry of palace-building by the maharajas. Indian princes were frequent travellers to America and Europe, where they visited the great aristocratic houses of Britain and France and found inspiration in an eclectic mixture of styles, from French château to art deco. Other edifices, such as the Udai Bilas Palace on the shores of Lake Gaibsagar at Dungarpur, some two and a half hours' drive south of Udaipur, adopted the Indo-Saracenic style, a distinctive fusion of British and Indian architectural elements.

Built in the late nineteenth century as a single wing along the lakeside, the palace was modernized and extended on three sides in the 1940s to form the present courtyard plan. All the interiors were newly decorated on the cusp between the Edwardian and art deco styles, yet there was also room for pure Rajput decoration in the form of painted glass panels and exquisite glass inlay, among the finest to be found in Rajasthan. All the rooms are filled with Edwardian and art deco furniture and fixtures, and papered with 1940s floral wallpapers imported from London. The maharaja at that time, Udai Singh II, was comprehensively won over by the European lifestyle, and the magical Juna Mahal (old palace) was vacated for the new building, which had every modern convenience: piped hot and cold water, electricity, and above all space. Western-style bathrooms were created with smart enamel bathtubs and huge cauliflower shower heads. The concept of the dressing room was also incorporated to accommodate the fashion for European dress, and the durbar hall was replaced by a drawing room with Edwardian armchairs and sofas upholstered in 1940s fabrics.

Harshvardan Singh, the present Maharaj-Kumar of Dungarpur, has given up a hectic business and social life in Delhi and Mumbai for the tranquillity of Dungarpur and the company of his two labradors. Determined to preserve this excellent example of Indo-Saracenic and art deco style, he has been adroit in opening the palace to paying guests while also preserving its distinctive ambience. Maintaining the impression that the palace is still a private residence, he invariably invites his guests for a genial early evening drink in the great drawing room.

Forty-five minutes north-east of Udaipur is the small town of Delwara, overlooked by the classic Rajput fortified palace of Devi Garh, the latest addition to the growing number of fine palace hotels in Rajasthan, with a story similar to that of Neemrana. Deserted by its ancestral owners, it was vandalized and stripped of everything of value decades ago and abandoned to its fate. In 1984 Lekha Poddar and her son Anupam came across the site, and so there began an ambitious project to restore the skeleton of the palace to its original state in every detail. Local craftsmen and traditional techniques were used wherever possible, along with local materials such as Udaipur stone and marble. Restoration, reconstruction and preservation were the key words throughout the project.

Similarities with Neemrana or indeed any other fort project ended at this point, as the equipping, decorating and furnishing of the palace took a dramatically different turn. The Poddars were determined to create a maharaja's palace to suit the twenty-first century. As a result, Devi Garh is audacious and visionary. Lekha Poddar and the Mumbai-based interior designer Rajeev Saini have created an interior that fuses the past, present and future in a combination of the Indian spirit with a rigorous international minimalism.

White and green local marble has been used throughout. A point was made of using traditional methods to create clean, contemporary lines and unadorned surfaces. Each room is themed with a different semi-precious stone, such as malachite, cornelian, jasper, lapis lazuli or mother-of-pearl.

India has always been open to ideas beyond its borders, seemingly unhampered by the fear of losing its own identity, and Devi Garh is an outstanding example of this broad-minded liberalism. The palace finally opened its great spiked wooden gates on the eve of the year 2000. A majestic celebration of India's past, it also stands as an convincing welcome to the twenty-first century and to India's future.

above left The fortified palace of Devi Garh. Once a beacon of civilization in the wild Aravalli hills, it has now been restored with style by Lekha and Anupam Poddar.

above right A view from a rooftop contrasts the bright limewashed stone of the palace with the rough hills beyond.

samode palace

Samode Palace, forty-two kilometres from Jaipur, represents a distinctive period in the evolution of the fortified palace in Rajasthan. The arrival of the British brought a degree of stability to the region, and with this the need for fortification receded; consequently, the royal purse was free to indulge in courtly decoration and display. The formal reception rooms, especially the durbar hall and Sheesh Mahal (mirrored hall), are masterpieces of painting and glass work, featuring intricate geometric designs and an explosion of flowers, birds and figurative motifs.

left The grand durbar hall is the formal reception area of the palace, where in the past the Rawal of Samode would have received royal visitors, dignitaries and high-level British administrators. Few other interiors can rival the skill of execution and the ravishing beauty of the decoration. **opposite** The ceiling in the durbar hall is hand-painted and features geometric and floral patterns alongside portraits of nautch girls (professional dancers). **artwork** Detail of the border below the open shuttered window in the durbar hall.

left The elaborate quality of the painted decoration shows that vast expense was incurred in the various public rooms of the palace. The advent of the British secured a greater stability in Rajasthan, so that where previously money would have been spent on waging war or on defence, the palace exchequer was able instead to use funds for patronage of the arts. **opposite** In the hall behind the Sultan Mahal every surface has been painted: the ceiling has swirling floral motifs in a Dutch blue; the dado is decorated with pencil firs, mango trees and various species of garden birds; landscapes include detailed illustrations of sites of religious pilgrimage. **artwork** Detail of paintwork on the cornice of the Sultan Mahal.

above The Sheesh Mahal runs alongside the durbar hall on the upper level. The entire ceiling and upper walls are covered with convex pieces of mirrored glass. What would have been a dark space, has become delightfully bright, the myriad pieces of mirror playing with reflected and re-reflected light. The Sheesh Mahal also had a more romantic purpose. The Rajput men at one time spent much of their lives outside, hunting or protecting their families. Their lives changed in the 1900s as they settled down to more sedentary pursuits, spending more time at home rather than outside. Lighting candles under the mirror work in the Sheesh Mahal would create just the effect of the celestial canopy under which they used to camp.

below left The Sultan Mahal is a public reception area for more intimate gatherings. The silver furniture, sofas, charpoys and footstools were brought from Nepal and the dhurries and rugs were all locally woven in Jaipur. The walls are painted with flowers, bowls of fruit and scenes from religious mythology. **below right** The ceiling and upper portions of the decorative jharoka in the Sultan Mahal has been covered in mirrored glass and overlaid with delicate gesso tracery work. Not only is the jharoka a decorative focal point, it also practical, letting in light along the back of the Mahal. **artwork** Detail of a floral design taken from the dado rail in the Sultan Mahal.

above This small anteroom overlooking the durbar hall that is finished in monochrome, provides a clever contrast to the ravishing paintwork of the durbar hall, seen through the archway. The women of the palace would have used this room and the corridors running round the sides of the hall on its upper level to view the ceremonies and court proceedings below. **opposite** Detail from a dado running between the Durbar Hall and the Sheesh Mahal; a riot of colour, flowers and birds. In this desert region gardens were highly prized, also known as 'paradise gardens' they brought colour, scent and birdlife to the rugged surroundings. Great efforts were made to locate sources of running water to supply fountains, ponds and waterways, the likes of which can be seen at Samode Bagh. **artwork** An adaptation of a floral pattern from a pierced stone screen.

opposite and above left Gallery along the upper level of the durbar hall. The elegant proportions of the receding arches, enhanced by the curved ceilings, create an impressive gallery with views to one side of the palace gardens and surrounding hills and to the other into the central hall.
above right The mirrored decoration in the gallery alongside the Sheesh Mahal is a tradition that originated in Iran. Glass balls were blown and mercury poured into them while they were still hot; the balls were then smashed and the shards shaped to fit the design. This gallery and the adjoining Sheesh Mahal are among the finest examples of such glass work in Rajasthan.

neemrana fort

A fortified palace situated near the highway between Delhi and Jaipur, Neemrana was neglected throughout most of the twentieth century and eventually reduced to ruins. With at least two-thirds of it collapsed, bringing it back to life was a huge task which would have daunted even the most enthusiastic of owners. Through the dedication and determination of Aman Nath and Francis Wacziarg, however, the royal complex was re-created room by room, just like an intricate jigsaw. Together, they combed the country to bring together a fine collection of indigenous and colonial furniture, which is set in surroundings that are now refined, tranquil and monastic in atmosphere.

previous pages left The Malabar Mahal adopts a south Indian theme with striking carved columns in wood and hanging temple oil lamps.
previous pages right Years of meticulous work returned the once-dilapidated rooms to their former significance. Nath and Wacziarg's design ethos is simple: innovative in spirit and monastic in ambience.
artwork page 58 An example of a traditional Rajasthani hand block-printed design.

left Attention to detail extended beyond returning the architecture of the rambling building to its original state. 'I bought every single doorknob and handle,' Nath explains. The fort having been abandoned and comprehensively pilfered, every piece of furniture had to be brought in. Colonial furniture, which has been placed throughout, offers the greatest variety of practical designs, ranging through rattan-plaited planter chairs, desks, tables and beds.

left and below Not all the rooms are grand; some are small and intimate. Because the fortified palace has an elevated position on a hillside, the views stretch out across a farmed landscape. Few windows are glazed so light mosquito mesh fills the space and the natural flow of air around the hill passes through the numerous doors and windows. The wood shutter for the window doubles up as a writing desk.

opposite A natty travelling washstand from the colonial period. Once washing has been finished the basin is drained and folded away. The small water tank positioned behind a mirror would have been kept filled by household staff, but is now plumbed in permanently.

udai bilas palace

The Udai Bilas Palace on the lake at Dungarpur was first conceived as an informal weekend retreat from the large thirteenth-century palace of the Juna Mahal above the town. The original building, constructed in the late nineteenth century, was extended with three new wings between 1940 and 1944 to create its current form. Its decoration is an extraordinary fusion of Indian and European style, with British floral wallpapers and art deco furniture forming a contrast with the traditional decorative mirror work and stained glass. With one of the finest collections of hunting trophies to be found anywhere in the world, it is a beautifully preserved memorial to royal India on the eve of Independence.

opposite One of the most dramatic departures from the traditional interior was the use of mass-produced wallpapers, imported into India in the early part of the twentieth century. The English country flowers at first appear incongruous in a Rajput palace, yet they do reflect the Indian's love of flora and fauna, also shown in the carpeting. Only the pictures of Rajput princes and the white marble temple on the lake suggest that the room is an Indian one. **left** The crystal glass standard lamp in the grand entrance hall was imported from Europe. **below** The trophies in the first-floor vestibule are examples of many throughout the palace; in the early twentieth century the Maharaja frequently sailed in style and later flew to East Africa for shoots in Kenya and Tanzania.

right Painted decoration such as flora and fauna has the effect of bringing the outside gardens inside the palace. The coloured mica panes admit light while also softening it. The fineness of the glass work in the decorative panelwork belies the difficulty of working the material; the fragile glass is awkward to handle and each piece has to be cut with a diamond-tipped pencil.
opposite One of the main bedrooms of the palace, this is an example of the fusion of Western period furniture, art deco and Rajput interior decoration. The covered porch overlooking Lake Gaibsagar demonstrates the highest-quality Rajasthani painted glass and mirror work, which gives this riot of flora, fauna and birds a jewel-like quality. The floor of the adjoining vestibule, seen through the door, is covered in large tiles of mirrored glass. Western influences are found in the plasterwork of the ceiling and the cornice, also in the way in which the wall-space has been divided. The cabinet houses the radiogram and was also used as a bar.
artwork Detail taken from the coloured glass mosaic of the covered balcony overlooking the lake.

left Four details of the painted glass, mirror and mother-of-pearl work that are to be found on walls and columns around the palace. Flowers predominate along with parakeets, wild boar, crocodiles, insects, tortoises and fish. **opposite** The lotus flower is considered a symbol of divinity and purity, a perfect bloom that rises clean out of the muddy waters, reaching up to the sun. 'In the beginning were the waters, matter readied itself. The sun glowed and a lotus slowly opened, holding the universe on its gilded pericarp.' (Indian creation myth).

devi garh fort

In one of the most audacious projects in India today, the fifteenth-century fortified palace of Devi Garh has been transformed into a visionary minimalist hotel. Lekha Poddar and her son Anupam, working with interior designer Rajeev Saini, have deftly combined the Indian spirit with cutting-edge contemporary design. Minimalism has been tempered with the judicious use of colour, as in the bespoke Benares silk brocades and semi-precious stones such as lapis lazuli, malachite and jasper. The re-styling of the interior abandons historical reconstruction in favour of an imaginative projection of a maharaja's palace for the twenty-first century.

opposite The main public reception room was another example of decades of abandonment and pilfering. Once the fabric of the building had been rejuvenated, it was furnished to suit a twenty-first century, forward-looking prince. The lotus pattern, hand-woven in Benares, is a contemporary example of the old skill of brocade weaving.
left Wherever possible, architectural features were preserved, including the cusped arch (top left), the column and corbels and statue and jharoka in the dining area (bottom right). The contemporary table settings (bottom left) complement the period surroundings. An installation (top right) is dedicated to the great Lord Shiva, with an antique wood-carved head of Shiva and a series of brass tridents, part of Lord Shiva's sacred implements. **artwork** Detail of a repeat lotus design chiselled into the stone balustrade on one of the courtyards.

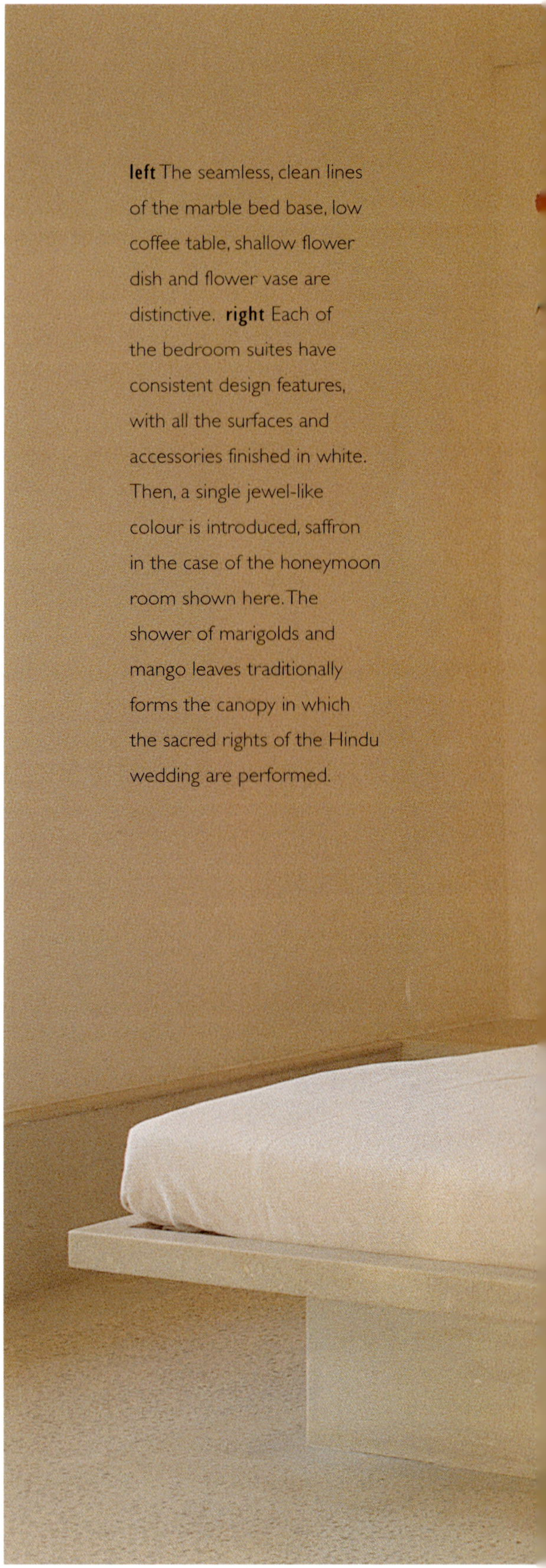

left The seamless, clean lines of the marble bed base, low coffee table, shallow flower dish and flower vase are distinctive. **right** Each of the bedroom suites have consistent design features, with all the surfaces and accessories finished in white. Then, a single jewel-like colour is introduced, saffron in the case of the honeymoon room shown here. The shower of marigolds and mango leaves traditionally forms the canopy in which the sacred rights of the Hindu wedding are performed.

below left Showing a floor detail in one of the suites. Sandstone has been exquisitely inlaid with green marble and mother-of-pearl, using the lotus theme which runs throughout the palace. **below right** Detail of a wall in one of the garden suites where a blossoming mango tree was formed with thick white marble in relief. All of the rooms have been kept spartan, therefore allowing single points of decoration to stand out dramatically. **opposite** The convex mosaic glass-filled niche is a traditional decorative technique that is given a contemporary edge when set within entirely plain surroundings. The white marble vases were commissioned for the hotel and turned by local craftsmen. They have a simple style, unadorned by ornamentation. **artwork** Detail of the lotus design as seen in the silk brocade panels in the durbar hall.

opposite An old royal elephant seat (howdah) with glass inlay and delicate relief work hints at the style of decoration before the palace fell into ruin. **left** The classical-styled chairs have been skilfully covered with hand-beaten metal, contrary to the traditional embellishing of surfaces with pattern. **below** The Mumbai-based interior designer Rajeev Saini has created a fusion between the spirit of India and cutting-edge contemporary design. The synthesis of original architectural detail, particularly the grey stone columns which surround this room, and the use of grey and silver contemporary chairs, is particularly harmonious. Numerous marble bowls were commissioned and here two elegantly cusped examples are filled with water, then sprinkled with pale pink blossom. Another example of the auspicious use of colour within a scheme dominated by monochrome. **artwork** A traditional representation of the sun god Lord Surya, taken from the howdah above.

tribal

| traditional huts | modern bhungas |

above left Muslim Jat tribal women collect water from a local well to take back to their homes. **above centre** Terracotta is still widely used for the storage of grain and water. **above right** A young Rabari girl is dressed up in preparation for a religious celebration.

artwork on page 78 Detail from the piece of Rabari embroidery on page 86. **previous page** Detail of the wood-carving on the shutters of the contemporary bhungas near Ahmedabad, Gujarat.

After fifty years of rapid industrialization and urbanization, India remains a rural society. Scattered across the subcontinent are areas still inhabited by poor tribal populations, generally uneducated and on the outer fringes of society. Although Indian culture has been continually exposed to foreign influences through successive centuries these tribal groups have tenaciously resisted them. Three groups of tribal homes are shown here, all from the state of Gujarat in western India. The Rabari and Meghwal tribal groups of Kutch live in western Gujarat, a desert region close to the border with Pakistan, while the Rathva tribal peoples are in eastern Gujarat, in the hilly district of Panchmahal. The Rabari are nomadic and pastoral, moving to wherever grasses are available for their sheep, camels and goats. The Meghwal have settled down to a degree; they still herd sheep and goats, but now derive their main income from leatherwork. The Rathva are agriculturists and forest hunters. The Rabari and Meghwal are Hindu, while the Rathva are animists. These contrasts between their environments and religions have directly influenced the style and decoration of the different groups' homes.

The Rabari and Meghwal live in distinctive bhungas (roundhouses), consisting of cylindrical, baked-mud brick walls topped by a cone of thatch, supported by a single central post. Such structures date back to the earliest forms of human habitation, as attested by the enthralled delight of archaeologists on finding evidence of a post-hole dating from thousands of years ago. Like other types of Indian tribal construction, these buildings are purely vernacular. There is no formal architectural input and the builders are the homesteaders themselves, who collect their materials in the immediate vicinity and use only natural resources such as mud, sticks and giant grasses. The Rathva live in a hilly, forested environment on the other side of Gujarat, very different from the Rabari lands. Their rectangular homesteads are made of bamboo and mud, with roofs of baked-mud tiles.

These contrasting styles of vernacular architecture have developed to suit the differing local climates, so that each type of dwelling is able to co-exist with its environment rather than challenge it. The structure of the low roundhouses of desert Kutch relies on the inherent strength of the cone shape to resist the force of the constant summer winds. The lack of rain – a mere eight inches each year – makes it practical to use mud and thatch, materials which help to insulate the inhabitants against the extremes of summer heat and winter cold. Structural strength is not a priority for Rathva houses, by

contrast, as they are sheltered by forests which protect them from high winds. Rain is the hostile element here, so baked-mud roof tiles are used instead of grass.

All three styles of tribal dwelling use mud. Plentiful, malleable when wet and strong when dry, particularly when mixed with straw and cow dung, it is an easy and cheap renewable resource. But it is now losing out to the growing popularity of concrete, a material with neither the properties of mud nor its aesthetic qualities. Sadly, the concrete box is increasingly seen as a status symbol among rural people, more desirable than 'inferior' traditional houses, so that many of the old techniques are disappearing. These changes would surely have troubled Mahatma Gandhi, who visualized independent India as a collection of villages across the subcontinent, each self-supporting with regard to food and inherited building skills. But as the tribal people, the principal repositories of mud technology, turn their back on their centuries-old expertise, many contemporary Indian architects and designers are waking up to and exploring the magic that is baked mud, thatch and wood. It is ironic that the element of urban culture that has been responsible for the gradual dilution of tribal building and decorative traditions should be the very one that is now helping to ensure the survival of such traditions.

One architectural team currently exploring this dying heritage is that of Nimish Patel and Parul Zaveri, who are based in Ahmedabad. Having spent years exploring and experimenting with India's building traditions, they have become passionate advocates of the appropriateness of mud for contemporary building and interior design. Putting their theories into practice, they have created new bhungas for a wealthy industrialist and his family seeking a meditative weekend retreat. Built near Ahmedabad with the aid of craftsmen and women brought from Kutch, the result successfully proves that mud and thatch are still practical and aesthetic. Faithfully following the interior layout of the original huts would have been too restricting, and a few concessions had to be made to the clients' understandable desire for a degree of comfort. Some of the huts were thus linked by a thatched corridor, tiles were used in the kitchen and bathrooms, and larger windows were let into the walls to increase the level of natural light and ventilation.

These new bhungas create the effect of a peaceful rural setting, far removed from the modern urban world. The interiors are a celebration of the rich and textural mix of craftsmanship that is so distinctive to Kutch. They also illustrate just how relevant the traditional approach can be to the contemporary world, both in design and in lifestyle.

above left and right This set of new bhungas built outside Ahmedabad follow closely the materials and structural traditions of Kutch dwellings.

traditional huts

The tribal people of Gujarat are remote from urban, indeed regular rural life, and their dwellings are diverse in construction and decoration, reflecting widely differing environments and beliefs. Three examples of such tribal dwellings are illustrated here. The bhungas (roundhouses) of the Rabari in Tunda Wandh on the Gujarat coast in Kutch have evolved to suit the hot desert climate, using only local materials for their construction, while the interiors are distinctive for their mud and mirror work. The Meghwal dwellings, also in Kutch, are similar in construction, with not only decorated interiors but also exteriors that feature bold geometric patterns, reinvented annually during preparations for the celebrations of Diwali, the Festival of Lights. In contrast to the Rabari and Meghwal, the Rathva tribes of Panchmahal have rectangular dwellings decorated with energetic and colourful wall paintings that illustrate the story of the 'Myth of Creation' and the marriage of Pithoro, the deity who protects the household from the vicissitudes of daily life.

opposite Many of the tribal groups in Gujarat live in bhungas (round houses). Traditionally made of mud, concrete is now becoming popular, which here forms the main structure. The woman of the house embroiders a blouse in the light of the doorway, often the single source of natural light into the roundhouse. **above left** The Rathva tribes live in the Chota Udepur district of eastern Gujarat. Their environment is forest and jungle, entirely different to the Rabari and Meghwal in desert Kutch, Western Gujarat. They live by hunting and gathering from the forest, harvesting fruits and edible roots. Here, a huge grain storage basket is being woven. **below left** A Meghwal woman sorts the chaff from the wheat in preparation for the evening meal. While the Rabari finish the exteriors of their homes with whitewash, the Meghwal paint the exterior of their homes with bold, naïve geometric patterns which are often symbolic. These same designs are frequently used in their embroidered and appliquéd textiles.

above left A young Rabari boy leaves the plain whitewashed roundhouses of Tunda Wandh to tend his sheep. **below left** Beautifully embroidered quilts incorporating mirror glasswork, done by the Rabari women, are neatly piled on top of the cabinets. **right** The distinctive mud and mirror work of the Rabari, here decorating the storage cabinets around the walls, are charged with symbolic meaning, warning of evil spirits or celebrating gods. The interiors are kept immaculately swept and the floor is frequently given a fresh layer of mud, particularly at festival times.

far left Detail of a camel saddlebag. **left** Detail of a small Rabari shoulder bag. The design is energetic, giving a colourful rendition of a festival, with dancing women and a caparisoned elephant. **opposite** The border of a tribal woman's gagra (skirt). Quilts, dresses, blouses and sack bags all form part of the woman's dowry and she and her mother and sisters will have embroidered many of the pieces. The embroidery and mud and glass work traditions are passed down over generations. **artwork** A detail drawn from the small shoulder bag above.

left The enclosed veranda of the Rathva house is coloured with naïve murals illustrating their 'Myth of Creation' and the marriage procession of their god, Pithoro, the tribe's agricultural deity. Alongside the procession are the tribe's ancestors, events from the living world, animals of the forest and ghosts. These illustrations have an energy and clarity that is similar to ancient cave paintings. **above** A large storage basket for grain and a carved column in the Rathva hut. The horses on the mural are a central theme in Rathva mythology, originating from a time when horse sacrifices were performed.

following pages left The high-maintenance, mud floor has been replaced with a dyed cement finish, which is snake- and scorpion-proof. The design is based on traditional tribal geometrics. **following pages centre** The roof of the bhunga is thatched and laid on a base of bamboo. Simple iron bars are installed in the windows instead of glass for security. **following pages right** Detail of a niche in the kitchen/dining area. Printed illustrations of Hindu gods and a saint stand alongside incense sticks. **artwork** Detail of traditional geometric tribal designs taken from the wooden bhunga shutters.

modern bhungas

Nimish Patel and Parul Zaveri have applied their mantra of 'simplicity and authenticity' to a set of modern bhungas built as a country retreat for a client in Ahmedabad. The use of mud and other natural materials of traditional construction has ensured the continuity of the old aesthetic sensibility and expertise. As with the homesteaders of Kutch, all the building materials were gleaned locally. Tribal dwellers were brought from Kutch to create the wonderfully decorative mud and mirror relief work. Parul commissioned special pieces of appliqué fabrics and selected textiles in exuberant, bright colours in order to echo the magnificent Rabari quilts.

left The relief work in the main living area is a combination of flower abstracts and geometric patterns. The low storage cupboard has a bamboo frame around which the mud and dung mixture is applied. The candles are know as arti lamps: tiny terracotta dishes filled with ghee, with wicks of hand-rolled cotton. **opposite top left** Detail of the mud and cow dung relief finish with inset pieces of mirror glass on the walls. **opposite top right and bottom left** Special pieces of appliquéd fabrics and selected textiles were commissioned in exuberant bright colours to reflect the magnificent Rabari quilts. **opposite bottom right** Detail of the mosaic tile splashback in the kitchen, the design of which echoes tribal patterns. **artwork** Detail from the mud and cow dung relief work in a modern bhunga.

revival

| amber haveli | pratima haveli | raj bungalow | dehra dun |

above left Chanwar Palki Walon-Ki haveli is built into the town wall of Amber, outside Jaipur. **above centre** Traditionally block-printed quilts are hung out to air in the winter sun. **above right** The architectural details of arches and niches are echoed as painted reliefs.

artwork on page 94 Detail from one of the wood-carved façades of a haveli in Ahmedabad. **previous page** Detail of the hallway in a Raj bungalow, New Delhi.

Crumbling ruins are a common sight in India. To Western sensibilities, such decay and disintegration can be shocking, indicating an apparent disregard for the country's heritage and culture; but this preoccupation with preservation is principally a recent Western concept. The Indian preference is to build new homes to reflect the achievements and success of contemporary generations, rather than live in the shadow of former ages. This attitude among contemporary Indians offers a partial explanation for the decline of classic older Indian buildings, but not a complete one. Old buildings have frequently provided a source of materials for new ones, today's owners usually live in reduced circumstances compared with their ancestors, and properties suffer from inevitable neglect as family feuds over inheritance – an all-too-common Indian pastime – drag on for decades.

While many Indians still consider that progress necessarily implies the rejection of anything connected with the past, a growing and prosperous middle class has brought with it an increasing awareness that the country's architectural and design heritage must not only be preserved but also revived. The projects shown here demonstrate some of the different directions that this spirit of revival has taken. Nimish Patel and Parul Zaveri of the architectural practice Abhikram, along with John and Faith Singh of Anokhi (the hand block printing company), have come to appreciate the genius of the builders of the past, whose work co-existed with the land and with the volatile climate. John and Kinnari Panikar, meanwhile, have pursued a personal crusade to save as many as possible of the traditional wooden havelis in the old city of Ahmedabad. Inside the home, an increasing interest in ephemeral objects from the past is evident in the collections of Bikram Grewal, which include antique Indian objects from enamelware to four-poster beds and botanical lithographs, while India's rich heritage of designs is being reinterpreted by top Delhi interior decorator and designer Raseel Gujral Ansal.

The great fortified palace of Amber, built to guard a strategic valley in the Aravalli hills, was abandoned in the early eighteenth century, when the maharaja, Sawai Jai Singh, decided to build the new city of Jaipur. The busy town of Amber that had served the needs of the citadel went into decline, and today its handsome havelis are fast crumbling away or lie in ruins. It was here that John and Faith Singh bought the Chanwar Palki Walon-Ki haveli, then little more than a carcass, during the quest for an old building on which

to demonstrate his joint belief with Patel and Zaveri that traditional techniques and materials are still a practical option for today. Having bought the haveli he worked on the project, together with Nimish Patel and Parul Zaveri who had first come across the building,

Determined to prove that continuity with the past did not mean stagnation, and that the revival of these old properties was a realistic proposition, they laid down strict parameters. They would use traditional materials and technologies and local builders and craftsmen, who would be fully involved in all decisions. The result is a handsome testament to the original owner's skill in combining taste with practicality, and an architectural and visual triumph. When work began on the restoration of the dilapidated property, minimal evidence of this remained. Fifty workers were employed over a period of several years to re-create the structure; as John Singh recalls 'I don't think anyone builds using local materials and traditional techniques except damn fools like us.' His determination to see this through has set the standard for other revival projects.

High walls shade the courtyards from the midday sun, and the dusky blue-green columns – stucco plastered with a traditional mixture known as aaraish, created by soaking kali (crushed seashells) with yoghurt and crystallized sugar in earthenware pots for a year – remain cool and as smooth as fine marble. Both internal and external decoration echoes the architecture in a series of shallow reliefs suggesting cusped archways and decorative wall plaques, interspersed with decorative niches that would have been used for household objects such as lamps and porcelain. Corbels and cornices have delicate floral motifs painted over the terracotta wash now traditional to Jaipur, and which has earned it the name 'Pink City'.

The half-timbered Pratima haveli is one of many such historic buildings in the old quarter of Ahmedabad. Kinnari Panikar's family have lived here continuously since it was built nearly four centuries ago, and when she and her husband John decided to buy it they had to negotiate with four quarrelling uncles, who met their plans to live in this 'run-down, no-go area' with consternation and derision. Many people are leaving the polluted and dirty old city and, as if to prove the point, the haveli had deteriorated into an appalling state: a depressing series of poky partitioned spaces with floors covered in tired linoleum and walls painted in gaudy high-gloss colours, all lit throughout by the acid-green glow of fluorescent strip lighting.

above left The inner couryard of Pratima haveli has recently been restored. **above centre** A view of the front of Pratima haveli showing the carved wood columns and façade. **above right** A small courtyard within the haveli.

above left A detail of the colonnaded veranda of a Lutyens-style Raj bungalow in New Delhi. **above right** The fireplace of the guest bedroom lends a distinctive Edwardian feel to the room.

As soon as John and Kinnari got their hands on the property their next task was to set about dismantling the years of ugly additions, scouring the city's architectural salvage yards and antique outlets for appropriate furniture and even original features that had been sold off over the years. Layers of paint were stripped from the teak that had originally been brought all the way from Thailand, while nineteenth-century Italian tiles, the traditional floor-covering, replaced the linoleum. The traditional dried-mud finish was restored in appropriate rooms such as the bedroom, where it appears divinely incongruous against the trompe-l'oeil painted ceiling.

So many havelis are under threat from property developers that John and Kinnari have led a campaign to slow down, if not stop, the wholesale destruction of the historic area. In their determination to save what is left, they have put themselves at very real personal risk by frustrating and enraging the powerful property developers. The Panikars offer living proof that the inner city need be neither dirty nor polluted, and in the process have given many of its inhabitants the faith and confidence to tackle more of its restoration: the future looks a great deal more optimistic owing to their personal example.

Dehra Dun, in the foothills of the Himalayas, provides a perfect antidote to the teeming metropolis of Delhi, a six-hour drive to the south, down on the intemperate plain. Here, Bikram Grewal has adopted another approach to the spirit of revival through his interest in period furniture, textiles and decorations.

By his own admission there is nothing remarkable about the structure of this 1970s house, bought several years ago. Even in this short lifetime, the house had still been allowed to fall into disrepair, so when Bikram Grewal took it over, he had a great deal of work to do to make it habitable. Apart from straightforward repairs he also enlarged the windows, added a bathroom and enclosed a narrow veranda that is now known as the 'sulking room'! The comfortable and congenial interior, however, has a very strongly defined character, reflecting the climate up in the hills, where in the winter the temperature regularly drops below zero. Such a wealth of fabrics, furniture and floor rugs would be out of place in the dusty, hot plains, but is eminently suitable here.

An avid collector with a particular love of colonial furniture, Bikram Grewal is an inveterate trawler of antique shops; he also attends auctions in Calcutta and embassy

sales in Delhi, while further afield the market in London's Portobello Road is a favourite. Grewal has several fine four-poster beds showing the British influence of the Raj. Botanical paintings, drawings and lithographs from the latter years of the Raj cover the walls, complemented by the fabrics, which in turn echo the lushly planted garden. A mural in the master bedroom continues this natural imagery while also disguising a set of built-in cupboards, creating an overall effect not unlike the hand-painted Chinese wallpapers found in British country houses.

This British-style informality finds a striking contrast in the regal manner of a colonial bungalow in New Delhi, with high vaulted ceilings and deep colonnaded verandas, originally built as temporary accommodation for civil servants of the British administration. The present owner, a member of one of India's royal families, wanted it redecorated to provide an appropriate setting for an exquisite collection of zardozi work (gold- and silver-embroidered velvets), family silver, portraits and furniture, and to this end called in the distinguished Delhi interior designer and decorator Raseel Gujral Ansal. Sympathetic to the period detail of the house and its contents, she decided to decorate it in a manner that echoed the sumptuous princely residences of the nineteenth century, while at the same time retaining the atmosphere of a home rather than a museum.

The main rooms were designed with high ceilings and low windows to keep out the heat, and consequently have little natural light. In summer, these rooms offer a welcome relief from the May-to-June furnace – cool, shaded and, above all, intimate. No attempt has been made to over-illuminate them: the drawing room in particular is a cavernous space, tempered by luxurious thick bands of stencil work at the top of the high walls and on the ceiling, to designs inspired by the rich ornamentation at Sikandra, near Agra. The effect of this is to enhance the feeling that the space is not unlike a beautiful jewel box. A deep veranda takes on the air of a very large room, especially when the rolls of chics (split bamboo blinds) are lowered. Here Raseel Gujral Ansal has chosen a combination of modern Indian metalwork and Edwardian wrought-iron furniture, covering the walls with broad alternate stripes of white and a dark golden sand colour, which recalls the Indian tradition of sprinkling water on the ground at dusk to damp down the heat of the day and which also evokes a unique and delicious aroma of rainwater on parched soil.

above left and right Bikram Grewal's house in in the foothills of the Himalayas. Running the full length of the building, this veranda provides an alfresco dining area at one end and informal seating at the other.

far left A colonnaded arcade faces onto the first courtyard of the haveli. High ceilings and the adjacent deep and shaded courtyard provide ample protection from both the harsh light and intense heat of the Rajasthani summer. **left** A niche at the end of the arcade has been converted into a shrine by the chowkidar (watchman), displaying present-day illustrations of various Hindu gods and saints. **right** Where there is no practical need for niches, walls have been painted with imitations. The entire haveli is painted in a particular tone of pink used throughout the capital Jaipur and which has given it the nickname of the 'Pink City'. **artwork** Pattern taken from the decorative niches in the haveli.

amber haveli

Painted in the distinctive pink associated with the royal capital of Jaipur, a few kilometres away, the meticulously restored Chanwar Palki Walon-Ki haveli in the small town of Amber stands out amid the ruins of other similar buildings. With the owners John and Faith Singh, along with architects Nimish Patel and Parul Zaveri, a master craftsman and local builders were employed over several years to revive this fine three-hundred-year-old building. With its cool courtyards, distinctive archways and traditional finishes, it is currently an excellent example of how the past can be revived successfully for present-day use.

previous pages left A view of the first courtyard; this would have been used to receive guests, conduct ceremonies and for business discussions with the outside world. **previous pages right** The decorated niches served various practical purposes: for lamps, for the storage of condiment jars and betel nut boxes, or for the display of decorative objects.

left This strung low chair has tribal origins, indicated by the roughly carved designs. The naïve fabric designs are hand block-printed in indigo by John and Faith Singh. Such old local furniture is often small and light – as with the charpoy shown on the opposite page – so it can be easily transported. **opposite** The haveli has been minimally furnished in order not to detract from the feeling of space. **artwork** Geometric designs taken from the chair back. The same designs are used by tribal communities in western Gujarat.

right The building design ensures that the haveli remains deliciously cool despite the midday summer sun. The stone floors always remain cool, for example, but they are also very easy to swab down, which is essential in such a dusty climate as this. Brackets, corbels and the corners of the ceilings have been painted in this public room with delicate floral motifs. The dado has been kept simple with black square outlines that accentuate the proportions of the room.

pratima haveli

Pratima haveli is a fine example of a genteel inner-city mansion in the heart of Ahmedabad. When it was built some four centuries ago, the intricate wood-carving with which it is decorated was a symbol of the region's industrial wealth. But, like so many others in the warren of narrow lanes and gullies of the old city, the haveli had fallen into neglect and disrepair. Saved from an ignominious end at the hands of ruthless property developers and restored by John and Kinnari Panikar with dedication and meticulous care, it has become an inspirational symbol of the successful survival of the inner city.

previous pages left The main bedroom with a naïve painting on glass of a local potentate and handmade, traditional sweeping brushes. **previous pages centre** Traditionally, bathing involved a simple bucket and cup standing on a small wooden stool, but this bathroom signals the arrival of the Industrial Age. **previous pages right** The floor-covering is a traditional mud surface, but notice the Edwardian-style chandelier and the trompe l'oeil ceiling of cherubs and Scottish Highland stags.

opposite A naïve children's toy: the emerald-green parakeet of India. **above left** Most havelis have a double-door system. The outer door is used when the occupants are in residence, the grills allowing air to flow freely. The heavy second set of doors are closed when the house is empty. **above right** The dilapidated tiles on the floor were replaced with nineteenth-century Italian tiles. **artwork** Taken from one of the tiled floors in a wooden haveli.

above A second bedroom in the haveli mixes the traditional and foreign – with the deck chair alongside the mattress and bolster cushions ranged in the corner. In the foreground there is a hitchkar, a recurrent Gujarati feature that helps to beat the stifling summer heat. Overheated victims drape themselves over the seat and flick the floor gently with their foot to create a refreshing movement of air as the hitchkar gently swings.

left A simple day bed and pillow for afternoon siestas covered in traditional white cotton sits in the ground-floor front room. The mirror reflects the serried ranks of wooden beams on the ceiling. The wood came from as far away as Southern India and Burma four hundred years ago. The glass pumpkin lamp is of a type found in many old houses across Rajasthan and Gujarat. **below** The kitchen area is part of the dining room. Black granite has been used to create the work surfaces. Brass utensils and storage jars are displayed throughout the kitchen, brass being the most commonly used material for this purpose. On the back wall stands an old samovar for dispensing hot chai (tea). Hanging from the ceiling is a metal basket in which fresh produce can be safely stored out of reach of the ants.

right Interior designer and decorator Raseel Gujral Ansal wanted to revive this Raj-period bungalow by integrating the old along with the contemporary. So the striped fabric on the Edwardian garden furniture is balanced with modern wrought-iron candlesticks. The stripe on the walls is a shade reminiscent of golden sand made damp by the rain. **opposite** Deep colonnaded verandas are the hallmark of the Raj bungalow and would have been used for coffee mornings and tea parties. The chics (split bamboo blinds) are also typical of the period, essential for keeping the heat at bay while accommodating any favourable breezes.

raj bungalow

Built in the early twentieth century to house the civil servants of the British administration in their grand new capital, New Delhi, bungalows represent an important aspect of the history of Delhi and pre-Independence India. Their structure – with thick walls, high vaulted ceilings and deep verandas – is perfectly adapted to the climate. But they were not built to last, and only recently – with many now in a state of disrepair – has a realization dawned of their importance as a record of a vanished way of life. Designer Raseel Gujral Ansal of Casa Paradox has illustrated how effectively such an interior can be transformed into a small but sumptuous jewel box, unashamedly celebrating past splendours.

opposite above left The wall-hanging shown here is an exquisite piece of Moghal silk embroidery. **opposite above right** The majority of the antiques and objets d'art are family heirlooms, but some are also sourced from contemporary European markets such as Portobello in London. **opposite below** The drawing room at the centre of the bungalow is protected by rooms on all four sides, including the deep verandah, so it is well insulated from temperature extremes. **right** The family has an extensive collection of silver heirlooms – a pair of ceremonial silver maces and an ornate, silver throne chair are included here. These items are combined with royal family portraits, regal furniture and zardozi (gold- and silver-embroidered velvets) to echo the sumptuous decoration of the nineteenth century. **artwork** Detail of a stencil pattern by Raseel Gujral Ansal for the hallway and drawing room of the bungalow.

dehra dun

Dehra Dun, formerly one of the smaller summer retreats of the British Raj, lies in the lower foothills of the Himalayas, surrounded by wooded hills whose summits are frequently shrouded in mist. The interiors of this 1970s house on the outskirts of the town represent a revival of interest in the ephemeral objects of the Raj, harking back to the cluttered comfort of the British country house. Filled by Bikram Grewal with colonial period furniture, and decorated with floral fabrics alongside an extensive collection of botanical paintings, drawings and lithographs, it underlines a passion for gardening in a region with one of the highest rainfalls in the world.

opposite left Until recently an open veranda and now used for afternoon siestas, what is referred to as the 'sulking room' captures the warm watery light on autumn afternoons. The rocking chair is from the 1940s, made with single pieces of wood shaped by steaming. **opposite right** An early nineteenth-century print of a courtly scene is featured within the bed head of this elegant Edwardian-period four-poster bed from southern India. **left** Two Edwardian single beds have been artfully joined together to make a sumptuous double. A botanical theme is evident throughout, reflecting Bikram Grewal's own passion for the garden, as well as for botany and ornithology.

left One of the finds of which Bikram Grewal is most proud is the handsome Burmese trunk with its bulbous cushion feet, spotted by him when dining in a restaurant in Bangalore, South India. When he paid for his food, he also paid for the trunk. The planter's chair is well adapted for a warm climate as the rattan back does not retain body heat as would a solid, upholstered piece of furniture. In addition, its shape is perfect for afternoon siestas. A fine example of an eighteenth-century Kashmir shawl has been used as a bedspread. **right above and below** These bird details are from the mural painted by Alpana Khare which hides the cupboards behind and injects an element of Chinoiserie to the room.

modern

| john & faith singh | amit ambalal | jaya wheaton | palam margh |
| mallika sarabhai | munnu kasliwal |

above left Aam Niwas, the home of John and Faith Singh of Anokhi, Jaipur. **above right** Amit Ambalal's 1970s house rises dramatically out of the soil, a controversial building for its time.

artwork on page 122 Design taken from a contemporary painting of lotus flowers from Nathdvara, Rajasthan. **previous page** A mosaic illustration of a Cyras crane, the likes of which migrate through Gujarat from central Asia and can be seen in the fields around Mallika Sarabhai's country retreat in winter.

The modern Indian house, particularly for the urban elite, reflects India's willingness to mix cosmopolitan influences with its own traditions of design and decoration. Two of the houses here represent pure internationalism. Amit Ambalal's 1970s modernist structure by the French architect Bernard Kohn was ambitiously experimental for its time, using a combination of cement, iron and wood rarely tried before in India. Raseel Gujral Ansal and Navin Ansal's project in New Delhi, by contrast, was for clients from the Shekhavati region who wanted to follow the tradition of building a grand haveli to reflect their business success.

The homes of John and Faith Singh near Jaipur and Mallika Sarabhai outside Ahmedabad share an awareness of the great ecological value of traditional indigenous building methods using only local materials. A desire to escape from India's overwhelmingly frenetic and congested metropolitan centres has encouraged the popularity of the house on the farm, essentially a country retreat secluded in its own grounds. Two examples here are both from Jaipur: Munnu Kasliwal's recent, small country house, and Jaya Wheaton's family home from the 1950s, a time when environmental issues and the decline of traditional skills were not even on the agenda of builders and architects.

John and Faith Singh's farm-house is a permanent home throughout the year. Their aim was to merge the interior and the exterior, setting ponds, courtyards and verandas at the heart of the building. As with their haveli at Amber, the entire project was to be carried out using traditional materials, technologies and skills.

The land had been used for growing wheat until John planted groves of mango trees. When building began in the late 1980s, the plan of the house evolved partly as a result of the mango trees, none of which was to be sacrificed. Faith imposed her own special emphasis, wanting to make the most of the Indian sunlight, which sends gilded shafts through the house at sunrise and sunset. When the sun is higher and hotter, it is filtered by intricately pierced stone jalis (screens). Skilfully positioned lily ponds also reflect light inwards, creating soothing rippling effects on walls and ceilings. Throughout the house, stained-glass motifs set high in the walls and inspired by the traditional use of coloured glass, throw subtly changing patterns of diffused colours onto the floors and walls.

It is hard to believe that the house once stood in open wilderness. Over the past fifty years, the city has flowed out to envelop the Wheaton house and far beyond it, and the

house now stands like an island, representing a more bucolic way of life. Amit Ambalal's house in Ahmedabad, also originally built in a rural setting, is now similarly embraced by urban sprawl.

Born into one of the great cotton-baron families of Ahmedabad, Amit Ambalal has continued the tradition of forward-looking liberalism that has distinguished the city's industrialists over the centuries. He demonstrated his spirit for experimentation and his faith in the future by employing the modernist architect Bernard Kohn to design a new family home for him in the 1970s. The initial premise for the project was again the need to escape the city, but it was also part of an explicit internationalism, itself part of the psychology of post-Independence India. Amit, himself one of India's most celebrated post-Independence painters, is influenced in his work by the Russian literary giants Chekhov and Turgenev.

The building caused a huge stir in the city that is home to India's most distinguished school of architecture and design. Why did he choose a foreign architect? Bernard Kohn had thrown down the gauntlet: if Amit had the courage, he could design for him a contemporary space in a modular form that would both meet all his needs and, most important of all, be sensitive to the strong Indian tradition of the extended family. Ignoring all criticism, Amit took up the challenge.

The interior of the house is dominated by works of art. Amit developed a passion for collecting at an early age, and now has many fine pieces of stone statuary and bronze, as well as the finest and most comprehensive collection of Nathdvara paintings in the world. In 1986 he built a studio in the garden as a private space for his own painting, using materials from a four-hundred-year-old haveli that had been knocked down in the city.

The Wheaton house was built as a modern bungalow arranged according to traditional principles: a big open courtyard exposed to the sky which was the centre of family life, and a social area where the cooking was done. In the 1980s, Jaya added a first floor in order to create a painting studio, and modernized the building to incorporate domestic changes and Western influences, including a refrigerator, a cooker and a dining-room table. Today, the interior is dominated by her own paintings, depicting images and people of traditional Rajasthan. These pictures complement her own extensive collection of textiles and antiques, the colours and textures of which in turn provide

above left an antique carriage in the carport to Amit Ambalal's home. The old wood structure contrasts with the minimal concrete design of the building.
above right The living room of artist Jaya Rastogi Wheaton, which is dominated by her paintings based on rural Rajasthan images.

above left Raseel Gujral Ansal and Navin Ansal gave their client at Palam Margh, New Delhi, a pared-down, international look inspired by art deco. **above right** A set of naïve sculptures reminiscent of migrant storks in the garden of Mallika Sarabhai's country retreat in Gujarat.

inspiration for her art. She also collects tribal silver jewellery and everyday objects such as brass thalis and katoris (eating trays and bowls), loving the simplicity of their shape and techniques.

Other projects are more extrovert and cosmopolitan. Casa Paradox, run by Raseel Gujral Ansal with her husband and business partner Navin Ansal, challenges the Western-inspired 'shabby chic' trend ('We are tired of shabby chic, we're surrounded by it!') with an urban internationalism that is fostering the development of a distinctly Indian post-Independence language of design and decoration. Favouring the assimilation of cosmopolitan ideas without rejecting Indian roots, it is a movement that can be seen at work in their latest project in Delhi for a leading Marwari businessman.

This grand Delhi town house illustrates perfectly the continuation of the traditional 'showcase' culture of the Marwari business community, adapted to suit early twenty-first-century aspirations, practical needs and comforts. The interior was designed as a free-flowing series of spaces, with furnishings and designs referring subtly back to the art deco style: certainly not cluttered, but comfortable, contemporary and chic.

Mallika Sarabhai's isolated farm retreat is rigorously minimalist in concept and function – a place for meditation and the enjoyment of nature – but it also had to be a comfortable, practical space that she could share with her two children and four dogs. As one of India's most distinguished classical dancers with her own troupe, media executive and spirited campaigner for causes including women's rights and environmental issues, Mallika urgently needed the privacy her bolt-hole provides.

Absolute simplicity was the keynote from the start: the house was to be as discreet as possible and completed on a restricted budget. Minimal plans were drawn up following the precepts of vastu shastra, an ancient Hindu belief system that aligns the inner self with the outer environment, in some respects resembling feng shui. Mud was used on the exterior walls, not only for its aesthetic qualities and because it integrates well, but also because it acts as a natural insulation, the circular indentations made with a vatki (steel bowl) creating shadows, so that only half the wall surface is in direct sunlight at one time.

A sunken courtyard is left open to the sky, in this way creating a chimney effect that helps keep the house cool, and also acts as a seating area when dry or a paddling pool

for the children when it is filled with water. In the evening, for decorative effect Mallika often floats flower petals and candles on the water.

In complete contrast to Ambalal's modernity is Munnu Kasliwal's farm-house near Jaipur, designed to induce a sense of gentle quietude in the face of India's headlong and enthusiastic rush to meet the challenges of the twenty-first century, and indeed the hectic pace of Munnu's own jet-set lifestyle. Joint owner with his two brothers of Gem Palace, one of India's finest and longest-established jewellers, he represents the youthful arm of the family, creating new designs which are causing a stir among connoisseurs in Paris and New York.

A major attraction of the site was its position among the Aravalli hills, providing dramatic views in one direction of the great fortifications of Amber and Jaigarh, and in another of a secluded hilltop temple. Kasliwal has created three separate terraces along the length of the building, the middle one raised by means of a traditional method of insulation involving earthenware pots and layers of stone slabs. He has kept this veranda uncluttered, with just two quilted charpoys that invite you to stretch out and stargaze into the wonderfully clear night sky.

The building is a series of extensions to what was originally just a simple cowshed. Local craftsmen were used on this project at every stage, and all the wood was sourced from trees that were felled around the building, in particular the eucalyptus that has been mistakenly grown en masse in India, in the process draining the land of its precious water supplies. These trees were replaced with mango and neem – the latter for its antiseptic qualities – alongside orchards of guavas, custard apples and pomegranates. The whole building is focused around outside living, with the surrounding garden – that is planted with jacaranda, acacia, morning glory and jasmine – flowing freely round the house.

As well as restoring the historic Chanwar Palki Walon-Ki haveli in Amber, Nimish Patel and Parul Zaveri of Abhikram, Ahmedabad, also work on contemporary projects, that are distinguished by their use of traditional design and building concepts. Their professional aim always remains focused on respect for ecology and tradition, but in contemporary homes such as those they have built for Mallika Sarabhai in Gujarat and John and Faith Singh in Jaipur, they have made a point of including some intriguing additional features.

above left The impressions in the mud wall of Mallika Sarabhai's home put part of it always in shadow, helping to keep the building cool. **above centre** Munnu Kasliwal's country retreat outside Jaipur has roof terraces at different levels. **above right** Simplicity is the decorative motivation for Munnu Kasliwal with furniture of wood, locally made wrought iron and plain cotton fabrics.

john & faith singh

The family house near Jaipur of John and Faith Singh, of the hand block-printing company Anokhi, shelters among mango groves planted and painstakingly cultivated by John. The house illustrates just how effectively local materials and traditional technologies can be adapted to a contemporary context, co-existing successfully with the immediate surroundings and climate. Taking advantage of the brilliant Indian light was of prime importance to Faith, who also wanted spaces linked with free-flowing ease. John, a passionate gardener, was keen to create a harmony between the interior and the exterior through an outward-looking design that keeps the profusely planted garden always visible.

opposite Faith Singh creates a collage of design and colour on top of an interior that is painted wholly in white limewash and distemper. The bolster cushions in the foreground take inspiration from tribal needlework. **below left** The new house carries on the tradition of the enclosed courtyard, but there are plenty of openings to the gardens beyond. **below right** Within the courtyard is a marble fountain that was commissioned by the Singhs. Deftly mixing old and new, the latter is represented by the beautifully carved pierced stone Jalis (screens). **artwork** Reproduction of an old hand block-print, Rajasthan.

amit ambalal

Leading contemporary artist Amit Ambalal's 1970s home in Ahmedabad has broken all the usual rules of Indian building. Designed by the French architect Bernard Kohn, it features a modular construction in cement, iron and wood which was revolutionary in both building materials and techniques. Today it provides a backdrop to Amit's remarkable collection of Indian art and sculpture, particularly his series of Nathdvara paintings of the blue god, Lord Krishna, considered the finest in the world. Parts of an old wooden haveli have been adapted to create his work studio, so bringing together the oldest and the newest of styles in one place.

opposite left The huge wood-panelled, pivoted door looks out towards the concrete portico and the garden. The rigour of the concrete finish is tempered by terracotta pots and abundant greenery. **opposite right** Detail of the small inner courtyard in the dining area. The courtyard provides essential light and circulation in this room at the heart of the house. **below** The dining arrangements are Western in influence, with the food being eaten seated at the table as opposed to on the floor. The manner of eating is traditionally Indian – out of thalis and with hands used as the main utensil. On the left is a Gujarati brass dowry chest on a stand and on the right an old black-and-white photograph of past Indian princes.

above left The chair by Axel Horn adapts a traditional bolster cushion to form the back of the chair. On the wall is one of Amit's Nathdvara paintings of the blue god Lord Krishna. The stone statue on the left is of the sun god Surya. **above right** In the centre of the main room is an old silver-plated temple stool supporting a temple tray. Above is a modern rug in blue, the colour of Lord Krishna. The rug below is in the traditional Persian/Mughal style. **opposite** The communal room shows Ambalal's varied tastes; in the foreground is a traditional India charpoy; along the back wall Western-style armchairs. **artwork** monochrome reduction of a Nathdvara painting showing lotus blooms and leaves.

opposite A contemporary piece of metal folk art, featuring figures of the monkey and peacock. **right** Ambalal has built a studio in which to paint. Situated in the garden, it stands away from the main building and provides a tailor-made space for his creative work. The wooden fabric of the building is decorated with intricate seventeenth-century wood carvings that were taken from a haveli in the old city which had been demolished. **artwork** Detail from the refined, wood-carved façade of Amit Ambalal's studio.

jaya wheaton

This family home was built outside Jaipur in the 1950s by Jaya Wheaton's father as an escape from the busy city. Modernized in the 1980s, with the addition of another floor to serve as an art studio space for Jaya, it is an intriguing mixture of old Indian tradition, new Indian ideas and Western influence. The artworks displayed on the walls present Jaya's distinctive romantic interpretations of Rajasthani traditional life, and are complemented by her extensive collection of exquisite village and tribal textiles, acquired during numerous sketching trips into the desert districts. The paintings and textiles both contrast with the contemporary furniture made by her son Samir Wheaton, one of India's leading designers.

opposite An outside seating area at Jaya Wheaton's home. Her collection of textiles displayed in all parts of the house was acquired through Jaipur cloth markets and trips to the villages, country fairs and local tribal areas. **left** Jaya's paintings have a distinctive figurative style inspired by rural life and tribal communities. Texture is integral to her work, with marble and zinc powder and smashed witch balls for the mirror work, which is also a traditional effect frequently used in interior decoration. **below** Many areas of the house include pieces by Jaya Wheaton's son, Samir Wheaton, one of India's leading furniture designers. The low table was designed by Samir and the chair was made for interior decorator and designer Ashley Hicks.

right The spacious quality of the building is accentuated by the free-flowing design. Walls and partitions have been removed and the maximum amount of light introduced. The grand staircase uses a glass balustrade rather than a solid rail, and features an art deco curve in the metal supports. The risers of the stairs are finished in black marble and decorated with the Celtic design of linked spirals. **opposite left** Raseel Gujral Ansal and Navin Ansal created a contemporary classic interior dominated by the gentle fluid curves of the art deco period. **opposite right** A pair of giant, organically shaped vases stand on a deep window ledge against a massive windowpane etched with random spirals, a motif that Raseel likens to fingerprints.

palam margh

This New Delhi home represents India at its most outward-looking. The house belongs to a family whose ancestors came from the Shekhavati district in Rajasthan and who have an impressive pedigree in business. As the grand havelis of that district reflected success, so does this home. Raseel Gujral Ansal and her partner Navin Ansal of Casa Paradox have created an interior that is both cosmopolitan and chic, using the traditions of Indian craftsmanship to produce a thoroughly contemporary feel, which complements some outstanding European hand-blown glass and paintings by the leading Indian contemporary artist Satish Gujral.

PICASSO
PICASSO
LEONARDO
MICHELANGELO

opposite A console table continues the art deco theme with a chrome finish and soft curves, topped with black granite from southern India. The glass vases echo the pastel colours in the painting by Satish Gujral, one of India's leading contemporary artists. **far left** The rounded form of the sofas and side tables in the drawing room are accentuated by the economic use of dark wood and fabric. The conservative use of strong pattern in the form of the Greek key provides points of drama. **left** The precise intaglio work in the black granite tabletop was undertaken by stonemasons from Agra. **artwork** Detail of the Greek key and olive leaf intaglio pattern from the dining-room table.

above left The walls of the entrance hall are finished in a subtle cream, which creates a dramatic counterpoint for the black marble set in the floor. A black granite tabletop is supported by a discreet iron stand, designed not to obscure the intaglio beneath. Another foreign symbol, the Celtic motif has been adopted here, in the candle sticks, glassware and furniture.
above right Tantric spirals were introduced into the surface of the sideboard, a cross-cultural echo of the Celtic spiral. The shallow glass bowl with floating gerberas is a familiar sight in the Indian home. **opposite** The juxtaposition of colour and tone has been used throughout to emphasize the shapes of objects and accessories: the matt-black finish of the softly shaped cat against a pale background; the clean elegant line of the chrome-finished drawer handles against a dark wood background; the metallic reflective surface of the candlesticks against the pale matt background. **artwork** The concentric spirals used in the glass window and sideboard top.

mallika sarabhai

Mallika Sarabhai's recently built farm retreat near Ahmedabad was conceived with the tender side of human nature in mind. As she is an inveterate campaigner on environmental issues, most of the house was made from recycled materials, while its energy requirements are provided by solar panels. Intended as a refuge from her demanding work as a dancer, publisher and media executive, it was built to a restricted budget as proof that an environmentally friendly house was both possible and affordable. It was also designed to have as little impact as possible on its surroundings, and so incorporates traditional tiling and mud finishes on the outer walls.

opposite There are windows everywhere, designed to admit currents of cooling air as well as heighten the enjoyment of the surrounding countryside, birdsong and garden scents. All the floors have been made with a simple, polished cement that is coloured with dyes. The quilted bed cover was commissioned in Ahmedabad, and the hand-woven rug was made in tribal Kutch.
below left Cushions on the bed, with typical embroidery and mirror work, are from Kutch in western Gujarat. The pastoral oil painting by Bharati Kapadia echoes the rural nature of the house and its surroundings. **below right** There is a consistent cool quality to this interior. White is used throughout and there is a pond in the main living area. The roof is made of wood; metal fixings would have been faster and cheaper but these would have radiated heat.

left and below The hitchkar is found in every Gujarati household. This example has a art deco design, evident in the back struts of the seat and the inset ceramic tiles. The hitchkar, which can be located either inside or outside the home, here hangs on the veranda where it can be turned to face either the house or the garden and fields beyond. **opposite** Heavy-duty chains are used to hang the hitchkar. Here, the brass has been cast with decorative figures and birds.

munnu kasliwal

Munnu Kasliwal has created a sybaritic balm for his hectic lifestyle in country retreat away from the bustle of Jaipur. As one of India's leading jewellery designers, recognized internationally, he has fashioned a space in marked contrast to his jet-setting professional life. Subtly simple, it combines the clever use of natural textiles with naïve furniture made on site, while the various rooms and terraces effectively bring the interior and exterior closer together. With its many roses and scented jasmine, the garden provides colour and perfume throughout the year.

previous pages The interior of Munnu Kasliwal's rustic retreat is unapologetically pared down. Colour and pattern is consciously avoided in the decoration, because Munnu feels that these elements can be brought in abundance from the garden, also assuring glorious scents. The large flagstones are locally mined and the low box is an old writing desk. Like the low table and stools, this represents the tradition of 'floor living' that is still integral to Indian culture.

opposite above left A beautifully woven charpoy bed base. **opposite above right** A collection of old brass utensils in the kitchen. **opposite below left** The only concessions to modernity in the house are electric light, hot water, a refrigerator and small fans. There is no air conditioning and no glass in the windows; simple iron bars replace the latter, ensuring a constant free flow of air. **opposite below right** The brass bathroom sink was beaten out locally by a utensil craftsman. **left** The natural qualities of wood and stone have a serene, grounded identity in this interior.

previous pages left The paper star lamp is one designed by Tom Dixon for Habitat. All the furniture, doors and shutters, were made from trees from the surrounding land. Trees such as eucalyptus have been replaced with neem trees whose leaves are soaked to produce a natural insect repellent. **previous pages right** This beautifully crafted charpoy, with lacquered wooden feet, was used by one of the maharajas of Rajasthan, when he went on shikhars (tiger hunts). An antique brass oil lamp in the shape of a parakeet hangs from the ceiling.

opposite left This is the only enclosed room on the first floor. The modern glass candle lamps are used on the roof terraces in the evenings. The shelves are made of stone. **opposite right** A butler's tray stands next to an antique copper storage jar, one of a pair, which would have been used for either water or grain. **left** In keeping with Indian tradition Kasliwal has used white and off-white cotton throughout the house and gardens. All the cushions and quilts are designed by Jaipur-based textile designer, Gito Patni. **below** Of the two terraces, one is covered, while the other is open to the sky and stars at night. Both areas provide bamboo tub chairs, which are locally made and finished in white cotton edging. The covered terrace is used during the day and provides useful shade from the sun. The roof is made with thatched grass, which is cut locally and bound in a traditional style by local farmers. In winter and on cold evenings, chics (split bamboo roller-blinds) can be lowered to close in the space, while the braziers ensure a congenial atmosphere.

sources

UNITED KINGDOM

Ananda Furniture and Textile gallery
24 Bond Street
Brighton BN1 1RD
Tel: 01273 725307
Fax: 01273 207474
info@ananda.co.uk
www.ananda.co.uk

Asian Decorative Arts
Christies South Kensington
85 Old Brompton Road
South Kensington
London SW7 3LD
Tel: 020 7581 7611
(oriental sales generally once a month)

Henry Brownrigg Asian Art and Antiques
Stands 2 & 21
287 Westbourne Grove
London W11
(Saturdays only)

Cargo
23 Market Place
Cirencester
Gloucestershire GL7 2NX
Tel: 01285 652175

Country & Eastern Ltd
8 Redwell Street
Norwich
Norfolk NR2 4SN
Tel: 01603 623107
(home furnishings, oriental rugs, ceramics, gifts)

David Edmonds
1–4 Prince of Wales Terrace
Chiswick
London W4 2EY
Tel: 020 8742 1920
dareindia@aol.com

Dyala Salam Islamic and Ottoman Decorative Art
174a Kensington Church Street
London W8 4DP
Tel: 020 7229 4045

Galeries Mirages
46a Raeburn Place
Edinburgh EH4 1HL
Scotland
Tel: 0131 315 2603

Galeries Mirages
646 Great Western Road
Glasgow G12 8RE
Scotland
Tel: 0141 334 8170

Ganesha
6 Park Walk
Fulham Road
London SW10 OAD
Tel: 020 7352 8972

The General Trading Company
2 Symonds Street
London SW3 2TJ
Tel: 020 7943 5332

John Gillow Antique Textiles
Cambridge
Tel: 01223 313803
(by appointment only)

Joss Graham Oriental Textiles
10 Eccleston Street
London SW1W 9LT
Tel: 020 7730 4370

India Jane
131–133 Kings Road
London SW3 4PW
Tel: 020 7351 1060

India Jane
140 Sloane Street
London SW1X 9AY
Tel: 020 7730 1070

Indigo
59 Walcot Street
Bath BA1 5BN
Tel: 01225 311795

Indigo
275 New Kings Road
Parsons Green
London SW6 4RD
Tel: 020 7384 3101
(Fine Eastern Antiques)

Malabar
31–33 South Bank Business Centre
Ponton Road
London SW8 5BL
Tel: 020 7501 4200

Monsoon Home
Head Office
87 Lancaster Road
London W11 1QQ
Tel: 020 7313 3000
www.monsoon.co.uk

New Rainbow Textiles
98 The Broadway
Southall
Middlesex UB1 1QF
Tel: 020 8574 1494

Oakley Shaw
93 Wandsworth Bridge Road
London SW6 2TD
Tel: 020 7751 0395

Opium
414 Kings Road
London SW10 OLJ
Tel: 020 7795 0800

Gordon Reece Galleries
Finkle Street and Kirkgate
Knaresborough
North Yorkshire HG6 8AA
Tel: 01423 866219
info@gordonreecegalleries.com
www.gordonreecegalleries.com

Revelloyd
272 Fulham Road
London SW10 9EW
Tel: 020 7351 2566

Siola
Market Hall
Market Square
Tremadock
Gwynedd LL49 9RB
Tel: 01766 514485

Brian Tapply Antiques
88 Portobello Road
London W11 2QD

Michael Telfer-Smollett Antiques
88 Portobello Road
London W11 2QD
Tel: 020 7727 0117

Titri
82d Portobello Road
London W11 2QD
Tel: 020 7229 2023
sales@titri-online.com

Trading Boundaries
The Sheffield Arms
Sheffield Green
Near Fletching
East Sussex TN22 3RB
Tel: 01825 790200

David Wainwright
18 Malton Road
Notting Hill Gate
London W10 5UP
Tel: 020 8960 8181

David Wainwright Showroom
63 Portobello Road
London W11 3DB
Tel: 020 7727 0707

Wigwam
25 Kensington Park Road
London W11 2EU
Tel: 020 7727 8888
info@wigwamdesign.co.uk

NEW ZEALAND

India Emporium
136 Karangahape Road
Newton Auckland
Tel: (64 9) 377 3733

Indian Wedding Supplies and Services
1a Buscomb Avenue
Henderson
Auckland
Tel: (64 9) 837 4122

Little India Ltd
1244 Dominion Road
Mt Roskill
Auckland
Tel: (64 9) 620 9106

USA

Kinnari and John Panikar
'Kinnu' (fashion and soft furnishings)
43 Spring Street
New York NY
Tel: (212) 334 4775

INDIAN REFERENCES

Abhikram Architects
15 Laxmi Nivas
Paladi 380 007
Ahmedabad
Gujarat
Tel: (91 79) 658 8018

Anokhi
2 Tilak Marg
C-Scheme
Jaipur 302 005
Rajasthan
Tel: (91 141) 750 860

Devi Garh Palace Hotel
PO Box No 144
Udaipur 313 001
Rajasthan
Tel: (91 29) 538 9211
www.deviresorts.com.

Gem Palace
Mirza Ismail Road
Jaipur 302 001
Rajasthan
Tel: (91 141) 374 175

Raseel Gujral Ansal
Casa Paradox Puc. Ltd.
A-574 Lado Sarai
New Delhi 110 030
Tel: (91 11) 696 8591

Neemrana Fort/Palace Hotel
A-1 Hamilton House
Connaught Place
New Delhi 110 011
Tel: (91 11) 335 2233

Samode Palace Hotel and Samode House Hotel
Gangapole
Jaipur 302 002
Rajasthan
Tel: (91 141) 632 407
reservations@samode.com
www.samode.com

Udai Bilas Palace Hotel
Dungarpur 314 001
Rajasthan
Tel: (91 29) 643 0808
udaibilas@yahoo.com
udaibilaspalace.com

above Two antique wooden dolls in a wall niche at Neemrana Fort, Rajasthan.
artwork on following pages From a wood-carved frontage of a haveli in Ahmedabad, Gujarat.

index

Page numbers in *italic* indicate captions to illustrations

author's acknowledgements

Yadavendra Singh, Samode

I owe a huge debt of thanks to those who introduced me to India and supported and encouraged me from the early days: Ramesh and Renu Mathur, Ajmer Alwar and Oman; Meera, Snehal, Ashish and Aditya Lakhia, Ahmedabad; Suresh and Rashmi Mathur, Ajmer and Dubai; Rear Admiral and Sundri Kapoor and Deepak, Delhi; Scylla Vatcha, Bombay; Sunita and Ajai Kumar, Varanasi; Mr JN Lal, Ahmedabad; Mr and Mrs S Nair, Ramnagar, Varanasi; Papaji, Rakesh and Papu Tulli, Varanasi; and Lady Meinetzhagen.

Thanks must go to those whose generous hospitality and friendship have made this book possible: Rawal Yadavendra and Arpana Singh; Raseel Gujral Ansal and Navin Ansal; Himmat Singh and family; and Bikram Grewal and Alpana Khare.

I would also like to thank the following people for their help, encouragement and assistance in bringing this book together: John and Faith Singh; Nimish Patel and Parul Zaveri; John and Kinnari Panikar; Maharaj-Kumar Harshvardhan Singh; Archana Kumari; Aman Nath and Francis Wacziarg; Munnu Kasliwal; Amit Ambalal; Jaya Rastogi Wheaton; Himmat Singh and family; Joy and Toy Singh; Lekha and Anupam Poddar; Mallika Sarabhai and The Sarabhai Foundation.

Also thanks to John Snelson for invaluable creative input throughout the project, especially on location, co-ordinating and styling and for his meticulous attention to detail and perseverance with my preparation of the text; Sarah Wicker for her co-ordination and great efficiency; Claire Wrathall who focused the original concept; and my editor Emma Clegg and designer Megan Smith at Conran Octopus for all their hard work, enthusiasm and creativity.

Henry Wilson is a photographer whose two passions are India and interiors. His work has appeared in many international magazines and newspapers, among them *The World of Interiors*, *House & Garden*, *Elle Decoration*, *Architectural Digest*, *National Geographic*, *The Observer* magazine and *Time Life*. He has undertaken a definitive photographic study of the city for the book *Benares* as well as having photographed Madhur Jaffrey's *A Taste of India*. His photographs have been used as book jackets for Anita Desai, Salman Rushdie and Norman Lewis.